Light Verse for D[

Dave Carr

A cold wind blew in from Siberia
Causing panic & general hysteria
Now it's sunny today
And the snow's gone away
Leaving me with a wilted wysteria

Best wishes
Dave.

Preeta  **Press**

Foreword

Welcome to my first published collection of poems.

Firstly I should say that I make no apology for mainly using traditional rhyme. Send the rhyming police after me - I don't care! I believe that rhyme works well with comic verse; even when the punch line is apparent the effect can add to the humour as I have noted when performing the poems.

My first venture into poetry was *The Horn of the Puzzled Rhino*, which is inspired by *The Green Eye of the Little Yellow God by* J. Milton Hayes. I was fascinated by the poem since my childhood when I saw Des O'Connor and Jack Douglas perform it as a comedy sketch.

I have experimented with ideas and various types of rhyming arrangements even to the extent of Rhyme Royal in the Letter to W. H. Auden, which is a pastiche of his own poem *Letter to Lord Byron*. *Mrs Isaac Newton* is a take on the World's Wife idea for which Carol Ann Duffy is renowned. *Pasta* was inspired by a spell I had working for a well-known tinned food manufacturer. *Blue Nun* was written as a bit of fun and I received a gift of a T shirt and bottle opener from the wine company, so they were clearly impressed??? *Respect for My Bitch* needs no explanation.

Finally I have sprinkled in a few short poems - which I hope will raise a smile or even a chuckle.

Dave Carr

Acknowledgements

should like to express my gratitude to the many people who have encouraged me to produce this book.

In particular my wife, Pat, who gave me the impetus to finally put the collection together.

I have been writing and performing verse for several years and have always valued the comments and remarks.

The group Write Out Loud has been an invaluable source of inspiration and feedback and I thank all its participants.

The Tudor House in Wigan and latterly the Old Courts have provided a regular forum for performance and I thank all those who have supported me there and at other venues nearby.

I thank Runshaw College (UCLAN) for the initial training in Creative Writing and continued support.

I am grateful to my friends who have read the poems and always had positive comments.

Lastly I should like to thank Rita and Paul at Preeta Press for the chance to publish this collection.

Previously published work I have only one poem *The Freckleton Air Disaster* which was included in a book about the subject by an American History Professor James Hedtke.
The book *The Freckleton, England, Air Disaster* was published by McFarland in 2014.
Some poems appear on the websites monologues.co.uk and writeoutloud.net

Dedication

For Pat

Published in 2018 by
Preeta Press, Bolton,
Greater Manchester
preetapress.com

ISBN:9-781999848934

Printed by Printdomain Ltd,

Contents

Papa Oscar Echo Mike

Mike was a Romeo, I met him one November
Looking for a Juliet as far as I remember;
He was a kind of Alpha male, who drove a Ford Sierra,
I prefer a man in Uniform but they're a good deal rarer.
He said he liked my dancing shoes and would I like a Foxtrot.
We checked into a cheap Hotel and soon he found my hotspot.
I read him like an X-ray, but he held me fascinated;
He could have won an Oscar, but the film would be X rated.
I started craving spicy food from India and Nepal;
I put on weight, a Kilo; that's not like me at all.
Victor at the Golf club said, "My boy you'll have to marry her."
Mike screamed and threw his arms about just like a Zulu warrior.
He said, "You see, I'm not quite ready yet to be a Papa."
I called him a Charlie and he called me a slapper.
But it takes two to Tango as I really ought to know;
I Delta blow for women's lib and told him where to go.
He joined a Yankee sailing crew, leaving for Quebec;
My scathing cry of 'Bravo' seemed to Echo round the deck.
He runs a place in Lima now, it's called the Aztec Bar,
Drinking Whiskey, playing cards – I said that he'd go far.

I'm Not Well

I woke up yesterday morning;
On my lip was a whole bead of sweat.
I read through my family health book
And googled the signs on the net.

I found lots of ailments in Latin,
Most of them too hard to spell.
I decided I had achalasia
And a touch of the anthrax as well.

There are signs of agranulocytosis
And adhesions are cramping my style,
With ankylosing spondylitis
Troubling me all the while.

Seems like I've got atherosclerosis,
The occasional anxiety attack,
And as if to add insult to injury,
I've got arthritis pains in my back.

I'm struggling along with the acne
And adenoid pains in my neck;
I'm sure I've acoustic neuroma;
My god! I'm a physical wreck.

I rang up and made an appointment
Next Friday at quarter to three.
I hope they can cure all my ailments
So I'll feel free to move on to 'B.'

Shakespeare's Car

Shakespeare's car had stripes across the bonnet
On alloy wheels were white walled Avon tyres
His pride and joy inspired him to a sonnet
You know the sort that everyone admires
He loved to take his motor out for drives
Cruising around at night with elbow out
Impressing wenches and some merry wives
A showman was our Will without a doubt
On the off-side sun strip was written 'BARD'
Emblazoned on the other side was 'BIRD'
'Tis said he used to park in his back yard
When working on his play Richard the third
And on the rear a sticker bright and red
'My other car doth be a Portia' it said.

Phone

Sorry I never called you
But my phone, it fell to bits.
I put it back together but
I'd lost the number six

I can call the curry house
To order vindaloo.
I can call the bookies,
But I can't call you

Perhaps I'll get another one
With camera, games as well.
But no. I'm quite attached to it
And so my love - farewell!

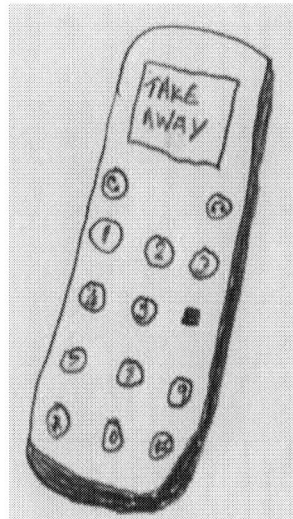

Seven Deadly Sins

Whilst contemplating, down the pub,
My New Year's resolution,
All in a flash it came to me,
I hit on the solution

I'm tired of trying to be good
They say that Who dares wins!
So this year I resolved to try
The seven deadly sins

I thought that to begin with,
I'd try a spot of LUST
I saw the barmaid's low-cut top
And peeked in at her bust

My face was stinging as I left,
And slowly wandered home.
Perhaps lust was a deadly sin
That's better left alone

So GLUTTONY, I can't go wrong,
I shouldn't need to worry.
I stopped off at the chippy and
Had fish, chips, peas and curry.

I've never had such problems with
My 'iron' constitution,
But now I had some doubts about
This New Year's resolution

Maybe GREED's more up my street;
That surely can't go wrong.
I'll sit at home and count my cash,
But that didn't take long!

I thought I'd have a day of SLOTH
And so I pulled a sickie.
I tried hard to ignore the phone,
Let's face it…it's quite tricky.

I didn't do the washing up,
I didn't feed the cat;
Eventually I just got bored,
So that's enough of that.

I got myself worked up with WRATH,
Aggressive and demanding.
I took a jumper back to Marks;
They were quite understanding

Ah ENVY; do not covet now
Thy neighbour's wife or ass.
But his wife's ass is something else!
She's quite a shapely lass.

I think he saw me eye her up,
He gave me quite an earful.
In fact he was extremely rude,
I'll have to be more careful.

I've had it with these deadly sins,
Though heaven knows I've tried.
I'm not cut out for being bad,
At least I have my PRIDE!

Medicine Man

Now gentlemen and ladies, could I just have your attention please,
I have a few things for you, if you'd kindly let me mention these.
I've linements, emulsions, compounds, antiseptic lotions,
I've got alkalis and acids; I've got anaesthetic potions,
There are tantalising tonics for your tonsil titilation
All are genuine, but please watch out for monstrous imitations.
Right here inside this bottle is the secret of eternal youth,
Effective either way it's for internal or external use;
Preventing symptoms of old age, you'll find it most expedient,
Developed by my granny with all natural ingredients;
She lived a life of vigor till a hundred and eleven when
Her hang glider was sucked into a seven forty seven engine,
Scattering her ashes over Derbyshire and Leicestershire;
She loved the shires, she'll rest in peace, of that we can all rest assured.
A spoonful every morning gives your joints a lubricating lift,
A spoonful in the evening helps your marital relationship.
It's so much more effective than most any other remedies;
On winter nights take great delight in rubbing your extremeties;
You'll find your brain is capable of Euclidean geometry,
Pythagorean calculus and complex trigonometry.
Two drops upon your pillow in a manner that you might inhale
Its vapour – in the morning you'll be singing like a nightingale.
Now you just might be thinking that it's going to cost you plenty – Did you
think I'd ask for twenty five? Well I'm not asking twenty quid
Because I'm in the neighbourhood and simply don't know when or
Even if I'm coming back, I'll let you have it for a tenner.

Out of Luck

I should have seen it coming when you boiled my rabbit's foot;
The bond of our attraction underwent a fatal cut.

My charm of St. Christopher – You know how much that meant;
It troubles me just how it got so out of shape and bent.

My lucky silver dollar's gone, replaced by eighty p;
A generous exchange rate, but it's not the same to me.

You little thief, you took a leaf from off my four-leaved clover;
I think I made my mind up then, our partnership was over.

Was that a magpie, one for sorrow, that you baked me in a pie?
I said it was delicious, but you'll know that was a lie.

My mirror's cracked from side to side, and up and down as well;
You've hit it several times with something heavy, I can tell.

You chucked my lucky horseshoe; it hit me on the head;
My luck's run out and so must I, before I wind up dead.

So when you read this letter I'll be well out of your hair;
I'm going to Mongolia, please don't try to find me there.

Call it superstition or just the seven-year itch,
But I really cannot handle being married to a witch.

Duncan Murray - A Cautionary Tale

Come hear the tale of Duncan Murray;
A man who loved the taste of curry.
He and his wife each Friday night,
Consumed a curry with delight.
His wife could only manage Korma,
But Duncan wanted something warmer.
All week-long Duncan would yearn
For curry night; Bring on the burn.

Soon once a week was not enough,
He needed more; He loved the stuff.
Balti, Rogan Josh, Jalfrezi;
The flavours drove his senses crazy.
For breakfast, poppadoms he'd crunch;
With onion bhajis for his lunch.
He brought home jars of eastern spice
And filled the house with sacks of rice.
He liked red chillies on his skin.
He cut them up and rubbed them in.
His poor wife was overcome,
She ran away back to her mum.
And when she'd gone he ran amok,
He wallpapered the lounge with flock.
With incense burning everywhere,
While strains of sitar filled the air.
Obsessed with flavours from the East,
He had become a curry beast.
But Duncan had a desperate wish
To make a giant curry dish.
He filled the bath with Vindaloo;
Tea lights below to warm it through.
Then right into this deadly gunge,
Brave Duncan calmly took the plunge.
And when police investigated,
They found poor Duncan marinated.
They covered up the bath with card
And took him to the town graveyard.
They dug a grave out extra wide
And lowered Duncan's bath inside.
"Ashes to Ashes," said the vicar.
"Cause of death – a dodgy tikka."
Be careful, or you too someday,
Could wind up as a take-away.
Reflect a while on Duncan Murray,
How he committed Hari Curry!

I Wrote a Line
(with apologies to Johnny Cash)

I keep my pencil lead sharp and very fine
I keep my notebook open all the time
One night I sat and stared from six till nine
In all that time, I wrote a line.

This bloody writing takes up all my time
The words go spinning round inside my mind
My brain is always searching for a rhyme
Because one time, I wrote a line.

I'm suffering a case of writer's block
I feel I'm always up against the clock
If I come up with something I'm in shock
Last night was fine, I wrote a line.

Perhaps my brain's gone rusty over time
I tried some WD40 mixed with wine
And tumbling keep the words now just out fine
Many's the time, I wrote a line.

Now I just sit here rocking all the time
I wear the straightest jacket they could find
And now my mouth and brain just won't align
They won't align, I wrote a line.

Mrs Isaac Newton

The pastry's rolled out ready
I've greased a large deep plate.
I'm running out of time now
The guests arrive at eight.

I sent him to the orchard
To get apples for a pie
He's been away an hour now
So what's the reason why?

He's sitting down beneath a tree.
It seems he's in a trance.
He just can't see the gravity
Of my circumstance.

Bike

I see you've been out on your bike again
Said the woman who's worldly and wise
"Does my helmet hair give it away?" I said
No your forehead is splattered with flies!

Postman

Oh look! here comes the postman
With letters in his hands
I hope he's got something for me
More red elastic bands.

Pasta

(With apologies to H Longfellow)

By the shores of Lake Lambrini,
Near the foothills of Panini,
And the plains of Fegatini,
Through the valleys in betweeni,
Where the flowing Canneloni,
Meets the wandering Marscapone.

In amongst the Machiato,
Near the fading Tinto Rosso,
'Neath the shading of Lambrusco,
South of Castle Osso Buccho.

Here a local pasta maker,
Bought out by a corporate baker;
Reputation keeps it going,
Striving but the tide is flowing.

Now they have a brand new master.
In his office, white walled plaster,
Lined with busts of alabaster;
Wants to make the pasta faster.

On the floor they were aghast-a,
"We have always made our pasta
To our recipes down passed-a
But we cannot work too fast-a!"

"Things are changing," said the master,
From his room of white walled plaster.
"We must make the pasta faster,
So our rivals are outclassed-a."

So the master strolling past-a
Turned the speeds to very fast-a;
Higher throughput, faster pasta.
More cash in the bank amassed-a.

"Faster faster!" screamed the master
From his room of white walled plaster.
"Got to make the pasta faster,
Jump to it you idle basta's!"

As the workers felt his blast-a,
They knew that it could not last-a;
Cogs were whirring far too fast-a,
Flying belts went whizzing past-a.

Soon the place was filled with pasta;
In the office of the master;
Even on the white walled plaster
And the busts of alabaster.

Now that frantic stage has passed-a,
Packed his bags and gone the master.
Now they can return at last-a,
Once more making finest pasta.
By the shores of Lake Lambrini,
Near the foothills of Panini.

Lightmare

Well there's something strange in my neighbourhood
And there's something nasty living in my wood.
So I tiptoe round with trepidation
I'm a victim of my imagination.

I feel demons lurking in every room
Shadows flicker in the ghostly gloom
There's things going bump almost every night
In my world of energy saving light.

Acknowledgements to
Ray Parker Jnr for 'Ghostbusters'
Stella Gibbons for 'Cold Comfort Farm'

Do not bend forward in those jeans so tight
(with apologies to Dylan Thomas)

Do not bend forward in those jeans so tight,
Pale flesh that shouldn't see the light of day;
Lace, lace against your skin so soft and white.
Those perfect rounded squatting hips invite
My roving eye, lured in and led astray;
Do not bend forward in those jeans so tight.
Stretched denim curving, arcing out of sight,
With squeaking stitches pulled in every way,
Lace, lace against your skin so soft and white.
Hip hugging waist, cut low just to excite
With frills and panty lines all on display
Do not bend forward in those jeans so tight.
Battles rage inside; what's wrong? what's right?
Hot blood and seething mud pools boil away.
Lace, lace against your skin so soft and white.
So how am I supposed to sleep at night?
Disturbed, confused, my mind in disarray
Do not bend forward in those jeans so tight
Lace, lace against your skin so soft and white.

Pandora's Box

I'll tell of a greek tragic heroine;
She was known as Pandora by name;
A quiet lass who didn't go out much,
A bit like the Oh limpic flame.

Zeus had commissioned Pandora,
The first lady made from the earth.
He was really quite pleased with the outcome;
Far less messy, he thought, than a birth.

Some say that Zeus craved a companion;
Some say it was merely a whim.
Cynics say he created a woman
To do all his washing for him.

Now Zeus was quite lazy by nature;
Some called him a bit of a slob.
He'd built up six months dirty washing
And he couldn't face up to the job.

Zeus was tortured by ingrowing toenails;
He'd been meaning to get them all cut
He was suffering badly from bunions
And the usual greek athlete's foot.

The laundry task fell to Pandora,
On washday she opened the box;
She released a great fountain of evil
As out flew a torrent of socks.

A smell so pungent and noxious
Descended all over the world,
As the greeks came to realise the horror
Of the curse that Pandora unfurled.

Pandora was stunned by her actions.
She vowed "It won't happen again!"
She said "From now on you wear sandals,
You and all the other greek men."

A hole in the space time continuum
Was formed by the actions that day
To upset the sock equilibrium
So that socks can just vanish away.

And it's said that socks are like salmon
As back to their source they migrate,
Led on by some deep homing instinct;
Perhaps they are seeking a mate.

So next time you look in your sock drawer
And you find that there isn't a pair,
Take all your odd socks down to Pandora's box,
You're sure to find t'matching ones there.

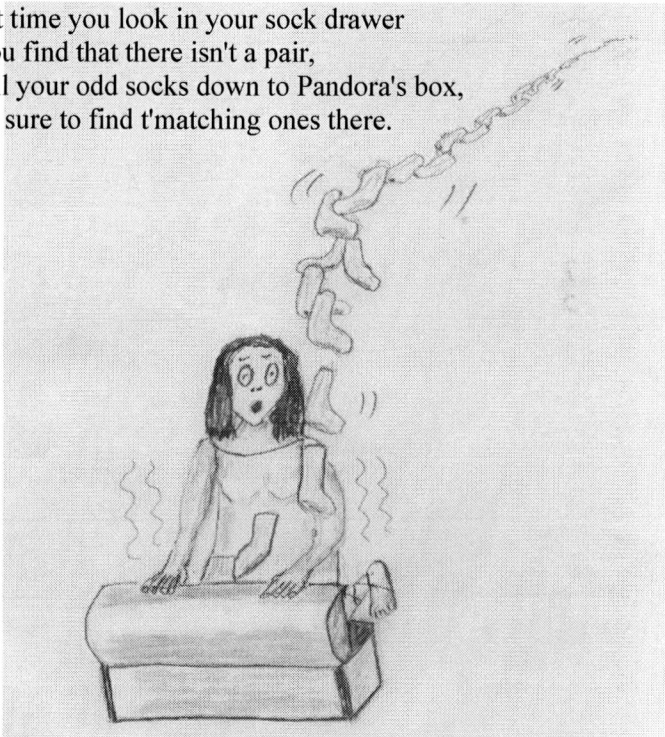

Bite the bullet

Bite the bullet, grasp the nettle
Pot is black as so called kettle
Ash to ashes, dust to settle
Heavy guns from heavy metal.

Down in the scullery, old wives bitchin'
Too many cooks in the brothel kitchen
Holes in time, no time for stitching
You scratch back when my back's itching.

Eye for eye and a tooth for cutting
One for all and all for nothing
If not iffing then effing butting
Even keels need an even footing.

Read my mind with a fat Braille finger
Love the song but not the singer
Har har har said Death's harbinger
Ding dong bell for a dead bell ringer.

The Prisoner

Can anybody help me please?
I live my life in fear.
I have recurring nightmares of
Being trapped inside IKEA.

I go in for a single bulb,
The sort only *they* sell,
And claustrophobia soon sets in,
My senses go through hell.

I stand amidst a sea of beds;
I'm spinning as I shout,
"I hate this place! I hate this place!
How do I get out?"

Hordes of frantic shoppers
With yellow shoulder bags;
Men with rimless glasses
Waving Swedish flags.

I dream that I'm surrounded;
Attacked by steel utensils;
Stabbed by shiny kitchen knives
And stubby little pencils.

Flat packs tower around me,
Shelf on shelf on shelf;
A whole lifetime's sentence of
Do it your bloody self.

Just once I made it to the door
And out - "Freedom!" I cried.
But then a giant meatball came
To bring me back inside.

I reached the final checkout;
On a trolley there I lay
In a self-assembled coffin,
 (A choice of white or grey.)

Prayer for Today

Oh Lord, forgive me nodding;
 My neck is out of joint.
I've got into the habit
Of prayer by PowerPoint.

Oh Lord, do you have broadband?
I've things I need to send
To illustrate my problems;
I'm going round the bend.

Oh Lord, where is your website?
Just give me a clue.
Surely there's a help page?
I don't know what to do.

Oh Lord, why don't you listen?
My life is in a mess.
It's fine for you in heaven,
With no e-mail address.

Superman Versus Villanelle

Strange happenings, some say too strange to tell,
A wicked woman stole a library book,
That enigmatic villain, Villanelle.

Poor Superman was held within her spell
And rendered feeble by this super crook.
Strange happenings, some say too strange to tell.

Tongue tied by a wrong-side, thong-thighed belle.
She bandied words and quoted Rupert Brooke,
That enigmatic villain, Villanelle.

But Lois Lane saw all was far from well,
Her Superman was dangling on the hook,
Strange happenings, some say too strange to tell.

Lois summoned from the burning fires of Hell
That green-eyed monster Jealousy, rose up and struck
That enigmatic villain, Villanelle.

So she was exiled, evermore to dwell
Within the pages of a poetry book,
Strange happenings, some say too strange to tell,
That enigmatic villain, Villanelle.

The Turkey
(with apologies to Edgar Allan Poe)

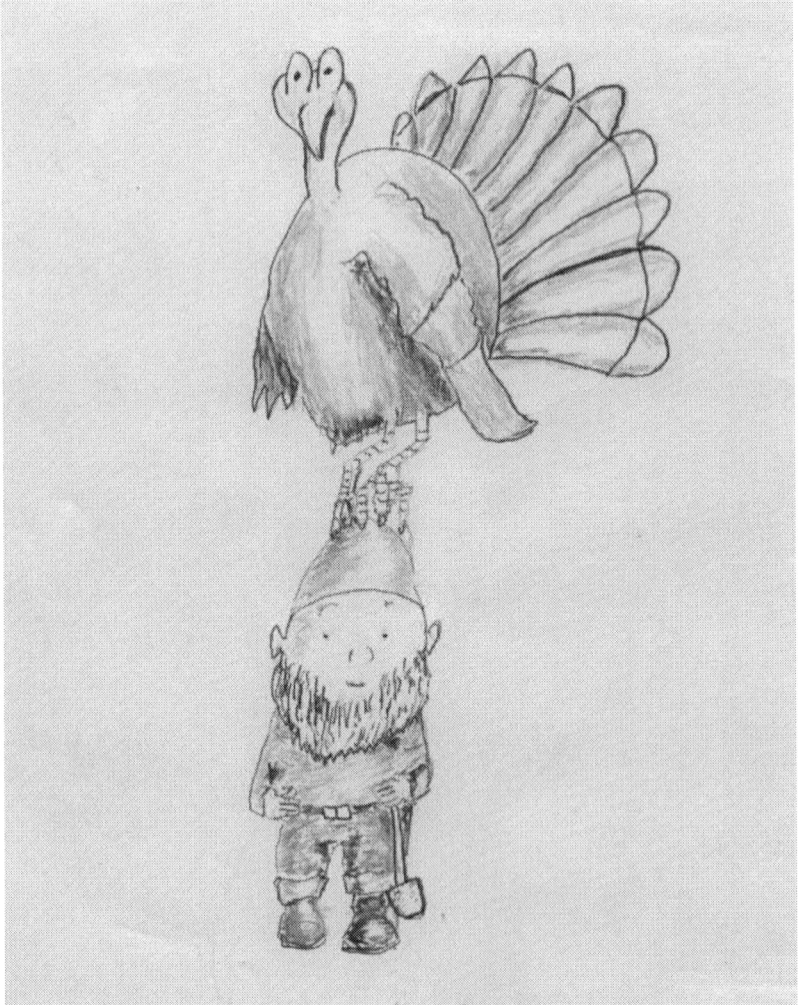

Late one night in late December, just how late I can't remember
Curled up by the glowing embers, watching Bond with Roger Moore.
Thought I heard a kind of glabbling, then again a blobbling, blabbling,
Glubbling, plobbling, blubbling, globbling just outside my kitchen door.
"Carol singers, humph" I muttered, "glabbling at my kitchen door.
Let's get back to Roger Moore."

As the glabbling grew stronger, I could take this crap no longer,
Dashing from my cosy lounge I hurled aside the kitchen door.
In the gloomy, misty, murky blackness I perceived a turkey
Perched upon a garden gnome and staring at my kitchen door.
"Tell me what on earth they call you Mr. Turkey I implore."
Quoth the Turkey "Neville Moore."

"Thought I heard my uncle Roger, maybe you could use a lodger,
I don't really mean to badger, I could kip down on the floor"
So I answered, "Tell me Neville, Are you really on the level?
Not a prophet from the devil? Just a bird and nothing more?"
Neville answered " I'm a turkey, nothing less and nothing more!
And besides, my feet are sore."

"'Tis with fear and great alarm, that I have fled the turkey farm
Sensed a great impending harm; couldn't linger any more.
They've bought themselves a cockatoo; We were at risk from Asian flu
So my friend I've come to you, glabbling at your kitchen door."
Thus spake Neville at my door. All the while my mind's eye saw
Steaming thick brown gravy pour.

Pondering my good fortune, I told him I would find some room,
"I can put you up at least until December twenty four"
I began to contemplate, the means to help him to his fate
Perhaps the axe or strangulation, but it shook me to the core.
Haunted by the thought of Neville dead upon my kitchen floor
Everywhere just blood and gore.

Bizarrely I grew to love him, couldn't shove him in the oven
I chastise him if he glabbles and he wakes me if I snore.
Now we're like birds of a feather, watching Bond movies together,
And you'll find we hardly ever mention Christmas any more.
Now I crave dead meat no longer, I've become a vegan bore.
Me and Nev for ever more.

Clown

I wandered lonely as a clown
With thoughts too sad to mention.
When all at once I came upon
A lonely clowns' convention.

Nightmare on Manic Street

Well since my baby left me
My life's been torn apart.
I'm down at the end of Manic Street
'Cos she stole the sun from my heart.

Custer's Lament

It was all a terrible mistake
As to Big Horn we went
When I said I could murder an Indian?
That wasn't what I meant.

Nursery Rhyme

Mary had a little lamb
And then she had some beef.
She didn't eat the pork because
It sticks between her teef.

Limericks

A scientist fellow called Pink
Invented invisible ink;
But he couldn't tell when
He had filled up his pen,
So he flushed it away down the sink.

There was a young girl called Natasha
Who one night encountered a flasher
She wasn't unnerved
As she calmly observed
My goodness me that's a smasher.

A young debutante from Prestatyn
Bought a ball gown made of satin
She went into shock
When it came 12 o' clock
'Cos it turned into coconut matting.

A gardening expert called Joe
Spilt potting compost on his toe
A geranium grew
Through the front of his shoe
And he won a rosette at the show.

A sensitive fellow from Bicester
Told his ex-girlfriend how much he'd missed her
Her laughter, her friends,
The romantic weekends,
But especially the nude games of twister.

The Horn of the Puzzled Rhino
(with apologies to J. Milton Hayes)

There's a stub-horned, puzzled rhino in the north at Chester Zoo,
There's a little marble cup, its contents gone;
There's a pining nymphomaniac sheds a tear for Rabid Stu,
And the stub horned, puzzled rhino grazes on.

He was known as Rabid Stu by the staff of Chester Zoo,
He was hotter than a rutting stag at bay;
'Cos if it wore a skirt he would woo and he would flirt;
And his conquests numbered many, so they say.

He had watched her from afar as she stepped out from her car,
She had parked between the reptiles and the bats;
And he planned to make a play by the middle of the day,
When she'd finished feeding her big cats.

She was by the lion's cage, she was nearly twice his age,
But he viewed her with a morbid fascination;
And before the day was done, they were both entwined as one,
In a shed behind the big cat's reservation.

26

She was mean, and she was wild, she was Aphrodite's child,
And it soon took its toll on Rabid Stu;
But she'd all sorts in her larder to revive his flagging ardour,
And on top of that she'd read a thing or two.

She fed him oysters every night, to keep his flame alight,
And it's rumoured she was sacrificing goats.
She served him steak tartare, and quails eggs with caviar
But she always made sure she had her oats.

For their love life to survive, she'd have to up his drive,
What she wanted was the famous rhino horn;
So she sent him out one night, with his penknife and Maglight
Then she sat down with a book to read 'till morn.

He returned before the dawn, and he clutched the bloody horn;
He was breathless, and his skin was black and blue.
His clothes were ripped to shreds as he collapsed onto the bed,
And his Swiss army knife was broke in two.

She took a hefty file and she struggled for a while,
That tough old horn was difficult to break;
But she ground the fetish up in a little marble cup,
Then tipped the lot onto a T-bone steak.

She propped up Rabid Stu and helped him to come to;
Then she fed him with the potent mix:
But he couldn't carry on, his will to live had gone
And poor old Rabid Stu was dead by six.

Some said that she was vicious, but she preferred ambitious,
For the way she treated Rabid Stu that night.
For no-one really knew just what killed Rabid Stu:
Did he die of love or did he die of fright?

There's a stub-horned, puzzled rhino in the north at Chester Zoo,
There's a little marble cup, its contents gone;
There's a pining nymphomaniac sheds a tear for Rabid Stu,
And the stub horned, puzzled rhino grazes on.

27

The Barbary Ape

There's a barbary ape who cuts my hair
And he makes me sit in a barbary chair.
With the sides hacked off and the back all square
It's a bit of a mess but I don't care.

Canned Philosophy

I think therefore I am.
I think I am therefore I am, I am.
I think I am a man therefore I am, I am a man.
I think I am the man that cans the can therefore I am that man.
I think I can, I think I can therefore I know I can, I know I can.
I think I can cancan therefore I know I can cancan.
I think I yam what I yam therefore that's all what I yam.
I think I am a can therefore I am.

Acknowledgements to René Descartes
To Watty Piper for 'The little engine that could.'
Also to Nicky Chinn and Mike Chapman for Suzy Quattro's 'Can the Can'
Finally to E.C Segar for 'Popeye's catch phrase.'

Mannequin

I'm in love with an M&S mannequin
With a hard-white stare and matching skin;
Now don't start screaming or panicking
'Cos I'm not a pervert or anything.

Her skin is smooth like sea washed stone,
Or a stainless steely feely phone;
Pragmatic without skin or bone,
To have, to hold, perchance to own.

We sat in Revive, in a comfy chair.
She was quiet, but I felt there was something there
I find it so rude when people stare
But I guess it's Per Una underwear.

I said, "Don't say a word", she didn't, bless her;
I'll have a chat with her window dresser.
I ordered cappuccino to try and impress her.
She left it. I should have got espresso.

I made up my mind. It was time for action;
I moved in closer, but only a fraction;
I stroked her arm to provoke a reaction
But I just couldn't get no satisfaction.

My wife's moved out as a disincentive;
She's talking divorce. It sounds expensive;
She said I'm obsessed, I'm just eccentric!
She said I'm possessed and I think she meant it.

I think we knew it would come to an end,
I'll still keep in touch but just as a friend;
I'll pop into Marks and Sparks now and again
Whenever they send some vouchers to spend.

Oh No - Another Ark Tale

They thought Noah was sick in the brain
When they overheard what he was saying.
"I must finish this ark
Before it goes dark,
As the weather man said it might rain."

Then a rustling was heard in the trees.
Noah thought it was only the breeze;
'Till he looked up and saw,
Coming in through the door,
Two bats and two birds and two bees.

Noah cried out "Any more!"
And a gibbon replied "Mr. Noah.
If you could just wait
For me and my mate.
She's ugly but such a good rower."

They were just casting off from the jetty,
When someone cried "Where's the yeti?"
Then running up the sand
There arrived hand in hand,
Just in time, two yetis all sweaty.

The problem with driving an ark
Is it's hard to reverse in the dark;
You can go without lights,
For at least forty nights,
Before you find somewhere to park.

The monkey was out of his tree
He said "This is not fair to me.
I know space is tight,
But I don't think it's right
To be sharing my bunk with a flea."

Noah called down to the shark,
"There's no place for you on this ark."

Said the shark, "You old fool.
Have you not built a pool?"
And he swam off to sulk in the dark.

Noah said, "Here's some friendly advice.
The toilets are not very nice.
Don't push for the loo.
Form an orderly queue.
And the elephants - please flush it twice."

After three days the weather was mean,
And the ark would sway, tilt and lean.
"Ewe!" a sheep cried,
Leaning over the side,
And a pair of chameleons turned green.

The yetis said "Don't forget,
We want to get off at Tibet."
They left on a raft.
Noah thought they were daft.
They're probably still drifting yet.

The woodpeckers started to peck
'Till they'd made a big hole in the deck.
A voice from inside
Said, "This sunroof's so wide,
It will let the giraffe stretch his neck."

The elephant went to complain
When his deck chair collapsed with the strain.
"Call this a cruise?
Just look at my bruise!
I wish now that I'd taken the train."

Noah woke up one night in his bunk
To the horrible smell of a skunk.
He swore, and he cursed,
But was glad, 'cos at first,
He'd thought it was something he'd drunk.

The giraffe said, "I feel rather daft;
But my neck's in a bit of a draught;
So I've knitted pyjamas
With wool from the llamas."
The hyenas saw them and laughed.

The penguin was sick of being waiter
He didn't get to eat until later.
They were always complaining
It never stopped raining,
He even snapped back at the 'gator.

They mixed up some food for the yak
From some meal that they found in a sack
They made a huge bowlful;
It smelled really awful
And all those who tried it said "Yak!"

Noah said," I've just checked the stocks
And there's plenty of food in the box."
Said the lion "Oh no!
If that really is so,
Perhaps I shouldn't be roasting this ox."

Noah sent out the dove to look round
And try to locate solid ground.
He brought back a branch
And some olives for lunch;
Noah said, "Just look what he's found."

Very soon the water had gone
And they all came ashore everyone;
But after the flood,
Noah never understood,
Where the two hundred rabbits came from.

Haiku

Roads to revision
Are paved with television
And good intendo

Had to say goodbye
To my tiny mobile phone
With a microwave

We're caught in a trap,
I can't walk out; because a
Spider wants his lunch

How hard can it be?
To research my bronchial tree.
Lung dark history.

Younger than today
Never needed older now
Won't you please help me?

Two chicken drumsticks
Rattle out a chicken roll
Paradiddle doo!

This sheep frightens me
Have I the guts to mount it,
Being a nervous tick?

I have a wetsuit
I wore it last Friday night
I have a lawsuit

Joku

Girl walks into a bar
Barman, gimme a double
So he gave her one!

Man Flu
(with apologises to The Clash)

DOCTOR YOU'VE GOT TO LET ME KNOW
SHOULD I SNIFF OR SHOULD I BLOW
PLEASE DON'T SAY THAT I'LL BE FINE
AFTER I'VE WAITED ALL THIS TIME
SO YOU'VE GOT TO LET ME KNOW
SHOULD I SNIFF OR SHOULD I BLOW?

IT'S ALWAYS SNEEZE, SNEEZE, SNEEZE
siempre achu, achu, achu
THIS MAN FLU'S GOT ME ON MY KNEES
manflu me tiene arrodillas
MY THROAT IS RED MY TONGUE IS BLACK
tonsillas throbbo pulsa paino
PAINS IN MY CHEST AND DOWN MY BACK
non sympathio cum ma wayo

WELL COME ON AND LET ME KNOW
me tienes que desir
SHOULD I SNIFF OR SHOULD I BLOW?
¿yo me sniffo o me snotto?

SHOULD I SNIFF OR SHOULD I BLOW NOW?
SHOULD I SNIFF OR SHOULD I BLOW NOW?
IF I SNIFF I GET IN TROUBLE
AND WHEN I BLOW I'M SEEING DOUBLE
SO COME ON AND LET ME KNOW

THIS INDECISION'S BUGGING ME
esta undecision me molesta
I'M WALLOWING IN MISERY
mi suffro molto fittu droppo
EXACTLY WHAT IS WRONG WITH ME?
me ruddy nosa com rudolpho

IS THERE SOMEONE ELSE I COULD SEE?
spouso hoho grandio joko
DOC YOU'VE GOTTA LET ME KNOW
doc me tienes que desir
SHOULD I HOLD BACK OR LET IT FLOW?
¿yo me sniffo o me snotto?
SHOULD I SNIFF OR SHOULD I BLOW NOW?
¿yo me sniffo o me snotto?
IF I SNIFF I GET IN TROUBLE
si me sniffo big peligro
WHEN I BLOW I'M SEEING DOUBLE
si me snotto video doble
SO YOU'VE GOTTA LET ME KNOW
me tienes que desir
SHOULD I SNIFF OR SHOULD I BLOW?
¿yo me sniffo o me snotto?

The Gnu and the Gnat

Said the gnat "How I envy you
For pronouncing the g in gnu"
Replied the gnu,
"If only you k-new,
For mine is a silent g too."

Well," said the gnat,"fancy that!
I'm so glad that we've had this chat.
So Mr. Gnu,
If it's OK with you,
Please address me as Mr G-nat."

Respect For My Bitch

I got a lot of respect for my bitch
She ain't no slapper
Or no rapper
She can't read no map or
Find her way round
Leyland
No way man
In the middle of the day man
But she scratch me when I itch
I got a lot of respect for my bitch.

I got a lot of respect for my bitch
She won't text, no
She's no techno,
Heck no,
But she makes the garden grow,
You know
I like to sit and watch her ass
Through my glass
While she cuts the grass
And strims the ditch
I got a lot of respect for my bitch.

I got a lot of respect for my bitch
She's a female
Without e-mail
But she likes real ale
and retail
She's canny
And so funny
Oh man, she
Never ever, ever carries money
But she makes me feel rich
I got a lot of respect for my bitch.

Blue Nun
(to the tune of Blue Moon)

Blue Nun
I saw you standing alone
Without a glass in your hand
Without a drink of your own.

Blue Nun
You with your sultry "Halo"
You stoked the fire down below
You made my glass overflow.

Blue Nun
Through alpine meadows we'll run
Communion out in the sun
Blue nuns just want to have fun.

And then there suddenly appeared before me
A multitude of dancing blue nuns
I heard the sound of music playing just for me
And when I looked again my dream was gone.

Blue Nun
I'll hold your candle for you
Walk round in sandals for you
I'd risk a scandal for you.

Blue Nun
I'd like to help you discove..r
Many new ways to love
But you said "Nun of the above."

And then I saw your mother superior
Standing in the shadows so blu
I confess I felt a flush of mass hysteria
'Cos I've got a thing about your mother too.

Blue Nun
I'm in the habit with you
I've worn your wimple. It's true!
Just something men like to do.

Blue Nun
If you will always be mine
I'll take you right up the Rhine
You are my favourite wine.

Letter to W.H.Auden

I write to you with reverence Mr Auden,
I seek the man behind the stone hewn mask.
A daunting prospect, say like climbing Snowdon,
Why set myself a mountain of a task?
Because it's there of course, no need to ask.
Of course with Snowdon, one can go by rail
Delivered effortlessly like night mail.

I've heard your life described as quite shambolic
Which, in the circumstances is unfair.
Being dead denies you of rhetoric
I'm sure things are much tidier up there
And even if they're not, I doubt you'd care.
Is there a corner where the poets write?
Or do you pester Byron every night?

More complex than Eliot or Larkin
Though some would claim far too erratic;
Perhaps you got complacent, lost the spark in
Later years - became less enigmatic;
Nonetheless the scholars are emphatic,
Fluent in every style and every form,
You took the literary world by storm.

Could your life have really worked in mining?
Another artist saw your true vocation;
Maybe saw your ragged soul was pining,
With radical ideas you fired the nation
Corresponding from war torn location
Picked to receive, it seems at random,
Such talent handed out with gay abandon.

A dizzy new world lure of city style
As war at home broke out, you broke away;
Such a public statement of denial,
Forsaking Blighty for the USA,
A tad unpatriotic some would say.
Oh! by the way, this rhyme royal stuff,
One line too many, or simply not enough?

You found a newer York as your abode,
You wrote of love, of politics, of time;
You wrote of England's backbone from abroad,
Drawn from old memories of northern limestone
Countryside revisited in rhyme.
Could you tell me please (if push came to shove)?
Did you ever learn the truth about love?

Out For The Count

My sister's halloween party
Was cancelled before the weekend
'Cos she'd cricked her neck bobbin' for apples
So I found myself at a loose end.

I thought I'd go hunting for vampires
Out in Transylvania they're rife;
And it's *the* place to visit this year,
I read it in Lancashire Life.

I knew I'd need stakes to fight vampires;
I looked to see what I could find.
I packed a few stumps in my sports bag
And a bat that Fred Flintoff had signed.

I flagged down a taxi in Chorley.
It was long and shiny and black
I said "Cabby do you know Transylvania?"
He whispered, "Aye lad, 'Op in t' back."

I got in alongside a coffin
I said "Am I having to share?"
He said "Don't worry lad, it's empty,
But I'll knock you five quid off the fare."

I studied him close in the mirror,
Which was hard 'cos he had no reflection.
I said "I never forget a face,
But in your case I'll make an exception."

He said "there's no need to get personal.
It's a long walk to Transylvania."
"Nay lad" I said, "Don't take offence,
I didn't think you'd mind as I'm payin you?"

The coffin were lined wi' red velvet,
Quite inviting - I fancied a kip;
And as t' conversation weren't sparklin'
I slept for the rest of the trip.

When I woke we were outside a castle
T'cabbie was nowhere to be found
But I noticed he'd left t'meter running
It were standing at six hundred pounds.

I thought I'd keep hold of my money,
So I wrote out a quick IOU;
And so as he wouldn't think me churlish,
I added a Euro or two.

Some Goths stood around in the shadows;
Their faces were ghastly and white.
I could tell this was no place for strangers,
Like Burnley on Saturday night.

At the door stood a wench in a nightdress,
"Am I keeping you up lass?" I said.
There was Meat Loaf playing on the hi-fi
Loud enough to wake the undead.

I said, "I've come to save your souls"
"Our souls!" she said, "No way!
But if you stick your neck out,
We might just let you stay."

There were ladies in white cotton nighties
All out for the count it would seem
I thought that my luck might have suddenly changed
But it's probably just that old dream!

They rose up and gathered around me
Pouting and fondling and kissing
I'd have found it all very erotic
If it hadn't have been for that hissing.

The brides were soon all upon me
When in amongst all the confusion
One of them sunk her teeth in my neck
For a quick DIY transfusion.

She said "I need your life blood;
A whole pint before dawn."
I said "Well, OK just a swift one,
But Dawn can go an' get her own."

One by one they all sucked my blood out
My poor limbs were feeble and aching.
I was too weak to get my hammer up
Never mind drive my stake in!

By now I was feeling light headed,
And I dropped down low on one knee.
I told 'em, "Normally when I give blood
I get offered a nice cup of tea."

They hissed and came slowly towards me
They were just moving in at the death.
I thought about calling last orders
When one caught a whiff of my breath.

I'd heard of how vampires feared garlic
So I'd had five or six garlic bread.
I blew a few kisses towards 'em
Then I sneezed several times and they fled.

A figure slid in from the shadows;
I ventured, "You must be Count Dracula."
He said "You can call me your countship
Or Drac if you like the vernacular."

I said, "Are you drinking Campari?"
As he drained the red fluid from his glass.
He replied "No it's just Bloody Mary,
She's a bleeding life saver, that lass!"

I asked "Have you not got a man's drink?
Like Lancaster Bomber on draught."
Count said "Are you trying to be funny?
Cos I think you'll find nobody laughed!"

I said "I've got a stake here for you,
You evil prince of horror"
He said "I've just had black pudding for tea
But I'll finish your steak off tomorrow."

I said "Excuse me for asking,
Which dentist did those two crowns?
I can recommend a good blacksmith,
If you're wanting 'em trimmed or filed down."

Count said "Now lad, I'm still thirsty,
And I do like the look of your neck.
Your garlic bread holds no fear for me;
Come along now - just a quick peck."

He drifted idly towards me
And held me transfixed with his eye;
I was just about running on empty
As his fangs started bleeding me dry.

It was then that we both heard a cock crow
And fear flashed across his red eyes;
We'd got carried away with the banter
And the daybreak crept up by surprise.

Quickly I pulled back the curtain
And the room was all flooded with light;
T' Count turned a peculiar colour
And started to tremble with fright.

I rummaged around in my sports bag
And said, "This is my kind of bat."
I hammered a wicket right through his chest
Triumphantly shouting "Owzthat!"

His face wore a puzzled expression
As he started to shrink where he stood
'Till all that was left was a cloak and two fangs
In a pool of half clotted blood.

All in all t'were an interesting weekend;
On reflection things could have been worse.
I had a free trip out to Europe
But I had to drive back in the hearse.

The Oyster and the Whelk

Said the oyster, "Do please tell, Mr Whelk, your curly shell;
 I'm intrigued as to how you got these whirls.
Ours have such an ugly skin, though the beauty lies within;
 Every now and then we manufacture pearls."

Said the whelk, "It isn't clever, it takes patience and endeavour,
 To accommodate my fast expanding figure.
I build a new extension, with an increasing dimension,
 So every year it gets a little bigger."

It was at the dégustation, they exchanged this information,
 Just before I slipped them down my throat.
Less salty was the oyster, though considerably moister;
 Perhaps a touch more lemon juice I thought.